Original title:
Blossom Ballet

Author: Franklin Stone
ISBN HARDBACK: 978-1-80566-647-9
ISBN PAPERBACK: 978-1-80566-932-6

The Flora’s Fabled Performance

In the garden's grand show, blooms wear their best,
Daisies twirl round, forgetting their rest.
Petals flutter like dancers, oh so spry,
While bees hum along, buzzing a sly goodbye.

Tulips trip over roots, quite out of line,
Grass tickles the daisies, making them whine.
Sunflowers stretch high, a comedic sight,
As snails slide by, in their slow-motion flight.

Blooming Encore Under the Sky

Under the sun's gleam, the lilies behave,
Swaying to tunes that they secretly crave.
A dandelion sneezes, puffs fill the air,
While the roses giggle, caught unaware.

Tulips trade hats in a flurry of glee,
Petals proclaim, 'We're the stars, can't you see?'
The audience of clouds chuckles and sighs,
As the violets wink, plotting silly lies.

The Whirl of the Water Lilies

Water lilies whirl in the pond's laughing waves,
A splash here and there, oh, the joy it craves!
Frogs join the fun with their croaking encore,
While fish perform dives, looking to score.

The pond's a stage, full of slips and slides,
Waving to the sun as it endlessly glides.
Dragonflies flutter, wearing flashy hats,
While turtles give tips on the best acrobats.

Serenade of the Garden's Pulse

In the heart of the garden, the flowers sing loud,
Chanting to the breeze, charming the crowd.
Marigolds trumpet with a startling glee,
As the lilac joins in, all full of spree.

With vines as their stage, they twist and they twine,
Bouncing in rhythm, feeling divine.
Each bloom a dancer, with hilarious flair,
In this garden of laughter, joy fills the air.

The Elegance of Growing Hues

In the garden, colors sing,
The daisies dance, oh what a fling!
Tulips turn to cheeky pink,
While daffodils wear hats, I think.

With every sway, the greens confide,
Giggles heard from bloom to stride.
Sunshine tickles, laughter spreads,
As petals hop on leafy beds.

Motion of the Blossoming Heart

A bud that wiggles, what a sight,
Dancing blooms bring pure delight.
Cactus winks in cheeky glee,
While roses blush behind a tree.

Bumblebees gossip in their quest,
Sharing tales of the flowers' jest.
Clovers play peek-a-boo with glee,
In this jolly, flowery spree.

Petal Dreams on a Gentle Breeze

Winds whisper secrets through the leaves,
While jolly petals prance like thieves.
A lilac tumbles, spins around,
Landing softly on the ground.

With every gust, a chuckle flies,
As butterflies wear silly ties.
Laughter blooms in every nook,
Amongst the flowers, take a look.

Spring's Elegant Flourish

In the park, a dance unfolds,
Petals whirl with stories told.
A rose wears shoes of golden lace,
While daisies join the fun-filled race.

Chasing breezes, the flowers tease,
A ballet of color, oh what a breeze!
With every bounce, they wave and sway,
In this springtime, jesting play.

Petals in Pirouette

A daisy spins with laughter loud,
Its tiny friends form quite a crowd.
They twirl and glide on the soft breeze,
While bumblebees do as they please.

Each tulip wears a silly grin,
As they attempt a leap and spin.
Their laughter echoes through the green,
A sight that’s simply too obscene!

The sunbeams chuckle overhead,
As lilacs dance without a dread.
With every hop, they sway and flop,
In this wild party, they can't stop!

As petals tire, they take a rest,
While dreaming of their funny quest.
Tomorrow brings a brand new dance,
For every flower loves a chance!

Dance of the Springtime Buds

In the garden, buds start to play,
They jump and shake in a quirky way.
With tiny twirls and giggles bright,
They steal the show in morning light.

A robin joins, all feathers fluffed,
With a flapping move that's quite unstuffed.
They all unite, a silly crew,
Spinning joy in the morning dew.

The wind joins in, with a playful sigh,
As petals fly and swirl up high.
It's a circus act, a floral spree,
Each bloom waving like, "Look at me!"

As shadows stretch, the fun won't cease,
For silly blooms, there's no release.
They'll dance until the day's all done,
And laugh about it when it's fun!

Whirls of Floral Whispers

A sunflower winks with a cheeky smile,
As violets spin and dance in style.
With whispering petals, they declare,
"A springtime dance? Yes, let's not care!"

They twirl around in a dizzy state,
Befriending insects, oh isn't that great?
With ladybugs and ants in tow,
It's a floral party, put on a show!

The air is filled with giggles sweet,
As every bloom finds its own beat.
From roses to lilies, everyone prances,
In this giggly game of floral chances.

As twilight falls, they know it's grand,
With petals tangled, they take a stand.
They'll close their eyes for a dreamy night,
And hope tomorrow brings more delight!

Garden Waltz Under Moonlight

Under the stars, the flowers sway,
As petals dance till the bright of day.
With a mischievous twinkle in their eyes,
They challenge the moon to join their highs.

A clumsy rose takes a wobbly step,
While violets giggle and lightly pep.
A garden twist, a floral dash,
As crickets chirp in a night-time clash.

The nightingale croons a lively tune,
While dandelions dance like fluffy balloons.
They jump and whirl, a charming sight,
In the soft embrace of the night so bright.

As sleep descends, they take a cue,
With dreams of dancing, under skies so blue.
Tomorrow they'll groove once again,
In this garden of giggles, where joy will reign!

The Rhythm of Nature’s Palette

Colors twirl in the breeze,
Painted leaves dance with ease.
Squirrels twiddle their tiny toes,
Painting joy where laughter flows.

Flowers giggle, the sun winks bright,
Bees bounce in a dizzy flight.
Nature’s laugh is a merry song,
Join the party; you can’t go wrong!

Butterflies in polka-dot coats,
Flit around like tiny boats.
Every bloom has a silly hat,
Balancing like a tipsy cat!

Oh, the trees wiggle their leaves,
With each gust, the laughter weaves.
Nature’s canvas is bright and fun,
Who knew joy could weigh a ton?

Budding Euphoria on the Wind

Dandelions toss their fluffy heads,
As giggles dance on playful threads.
A breeze tells secrets to the wheat,
While rhythm makes the meadows beat.

Robins chirp in a comic tone,
Tickling the flowers, they've overgrown.
Whirls of petals catch the light,
Spinning tales of a woeful knight.

Grasshoppers tap their tiny feet,
In a jazz tune, oh so sweet.
The flowers sway like they're in a play,
Laughing groups in the sun's ballet!

As the sky paints itself in glee,
Nature's laughter is wild and free.
With each bud, a chuckle ignites,
Springtime shimmies under bright lights!

Tapestry of Floral Footsteps

Petals scatter with sassy flair,
Each one wears a sparkly hair.
Blossoms trip in a gust of fun,
With every bounce, they've just begun.

Daisies in sneakers skip along,
Singing jolly, silly songs.
A rose gives way to a laugh,
While tulips pose for a photograph!

The sun winks at the silly bees,
Cheering each bumble with the breeze.
Petals slide in a jaunty race,
As giggles sprinkle the open space.

Through the garden, the mischief twirls,
Every flower opens and unfurls.
With colors bright and laughter sweet,
Join this dance, feel the happy beat!

Petal Pirouettes at Dawn

At dawn, the petals start to sway,
With morning light, they want to play.
A tulip leaps with a silly grin,
Flashing colors like it's a win!

Breeze whispers to each playful bud,
They giggle, leap, and even thud.
In this grand waltz, they twist and turn,
With nature's joy, there's much to learn!

Ladybugs join in the fun parade,
As flowers dance, they're not afraid.
Dancing under the yawning sky,
With every twirl, they flicker and fly.

A sunflower spins in a curvy spin,
Waving petals; let's all jump in!
At day's first light, the laughter starts,
In this grand ballet, we share our hearts!

Garden Gala of the Flower Fairies

In the garden, fairies twirl,
Dressed in petals, skirts unfurl.
Bees are buzzing, quite a sight,
Winging high, they join the flight.

Laughter echoes, leaves are green,
In this party, pure and keen.
Everyone's wearing grass as shoes,
The daisies giggle, they can’t lose.

Mushrooms dance like tiny men,
Wobbling ‘round like drunken hens.
Squirrels peek through blooming vines,
Judging moves and sipping wines.

Underneath a starry gleam,
They all jump and share a meme.
Each bloom cracks a funny joke,
As the winds start dancing, woke.

Whirling Flora in Twilight Grace

In twilight's glow, the petals sway,
With every twirl, they game and play.
Lilies leap in a gentle breeze,
Spinning 'round like fancy teas.

Bumblebees give quick, sly winks,
Their dance is better than it thinks.
While daisies giggle, moving light,
Chasing shadows, what a sight!

Tulip tops do flips with glee,
“Oh what joy to dance, said she!”
A waltz of colors, quite absurd,
With silly twitches, not a word.

As moons peek down with glowing eyes,
The flowers laugh beneath their guise.
In this ballet — oh, so grand,
With petals' pirouettes, hand in hand.

Rhythmic Blossoms of the Earth

In a field where flowers hum,
Each petal keeps a steady drum.
The daisies bounce on springy toes,
And tulips twist between the rows.

Crickets chirp their silly tune,
While nightshades sway to the moon.
"Look at that sunflower's dance!"
Said roses, lost in summer's chance.

A daffodil spins like a top,
Holding strong, it will not flop.
With every sway, the grass does cheer,
As bees buzz in, it's all quite clear.

This rhythm of nature's joyful spree,
Has every leaf dancing with glee.
A comic show for all to see,
In every bloom, pure jubilee.

Nature's Celestial Pas de Trois

Under stars, a dance unfolds,
A trio of petals, bold and gold.
With a flutter, lilacs take flight,
In the moon's glow, oh what a sight!

A rose spins with a leafy mate,
While twirling around, they seem so great.
The forget-me-nots giggle and sway,
“Don’t trip over roots!” they yell and play.

Ferns join in with a graceful bow,
Making it fun, but don't ask how.
With each bend and flip, they burst in cheer,
“Oh darling, watch that thistle near!”

Underneath the laughing skies,
They twinkle like stars, brightening eyes.
In this wild dance, they strive so hard,
These nature’s dancers with a funny card.

Poetry of the Springtime Stage

In the garden, tulips prance,
With daffodils in a silly dance.
Bees buzz around in a jolly queue,
Wearing tiny hats, quite a zoo!

Sunshine giggles, a warm embrace,
While petals argue about their grace.
A butterfly in polka-dot tights,
Twirls and tumbles, what funny sights!

Harmony of Nature's Palette

The daisies don a rainbow hue,
Playing dress-up, oh what a view!
Violets chuckle, leaning in tight,
Silly whispers beneath the light.

Painted skies with clouds like cream,
Birds all join in a feathery dream.
A squirrel, clad in a scarf so bright,
Jumps for joy at the sheer delight!

The Dance of the Pink Horizon

At dawn, the skies begin to sway,
As pinks and oranges join the play.
A cheeky robin struts with glee,
Winking at flowers, “Look at me!”

The tulips giggle, their heads held high,
While ants in tiny suits march by.
This silly ballet of soft and bright,
Makes each morning feel just right!

An Ode to the Blooming Figure

In the meadow, flowers compete,
Who can dance on the lightest feet?
Daisies laugh, spinning round fast,
Chasing shadows, a playful blast!

The breeze joins in with a whistling tune,
Encouraging petals to sway and swoon.
A caterpillar, with grace and flair,
Practices moves on the soft green spare!

Spring's Gentle Tapestry

A daisy wore a polka dot,
While tulips tried to dance a lot.
The violets giggled, swaying wide,
As bees in blazers took a ride.

The sunbeams dipped in golden flair,
And bunnies hopped without a care.
They twirled and looped in sunlit glee,
A joyous sight for all to see.

Oh, petals floating through the air,
Tickling noses everywhere.
A daffodil with hopes to sway,
Said, 'Watch me bloom, I'll win the day!'

As laughter ripples through the green,
Each flower knows just what I mean.
In this season's delightful tale,
Nature's strict rules begin to fail.

Twirling in Floral Dreams

Daffodils in tutus spun,
While ladybugs just laughed for fun.
A fragrant breeze, a soft ballet,
With petals dancing all the way.

A clumsy bee tripped on a stem,
Fell in a rose like a lost gem.
The daisies squeaked, "Get up, old chap!"
As he adjusted his tiny cap.

The lilies rolled in joyful play,
Creating chaos on display.
With every twist and every turn,
They shared the beauty they discern.

They followed footsteps of the brook,
In this wild dance, come take a look.
A waltz that flutters, lifts the heart,
A springtime show, a floral art.

Enchantment Among the Blossoms

In gardens where the petals prance,
The flowers join in silly dance.
A cactus winks, a pine tree sways,
As giggles echo through the rays.

The rose declared, "I've got the moves!
Come join my groove, let's share our grooves!"
And violets, cheeky, joined along,
Their rhythm ended in a song.

A bumblebee skipped past a sprout,
Who shouted, "Hey! Don't knock me out!"
But every bloom, both big and small,
Agreed that laughter beats them all.

With each new twirl, they spread delight,
Under the sun, so warm and bright.
Fluffy clouds became their stage,
As nature danced through every page.

Symphony of the Wildflower Waltz

The sun rose up, a golden queen,
Awakening the fields of green.
With giggles soft, the petals prate,
And start a waltz that's truly great.

Each daffodil with choreographed swings,
Swayed like dancers, with shiny rings.
They twirled and turned, each fresh detail,
As daisies rang the happy bell.

"Oh look at me!" the poppy cheered,
With playful jests, the crowd appeared.
The lilacs laughed, the sunflowers clapped,
In this wild show, no one was trapped.

Together in this flowered spree,
They painted joy with wild esprit.
For in this crazy dance of glee,
Each bloom composes harmony.

Impressions of Nature's Ballet

The daisies dance in pairs,
With antlers made of leaves.
While butterflies wear tutus,
In swirling summer heaves.

The sunbeams clap their hands,
While shadows skip and play.
The breeze, a playful partner,
Whirls the dandelion away.

The Ballet of the Budding Dreams

Tiny seeds in a pot,
Wiggle, giggle, sprout.
A cabbage does a tango,
While carrots twist about.

A tulip in a tutu,
Sways in a breeze so light,
While radishes keep rhythm,
In their very own ballet night.

A Whirlwind of Flora and Light

Petals pirouette softly,
Underneath the sun's warm gaze.
A fern does the cha-cha,
In this greenery ballet phase.

The clouds roll in like curtains,
As raindrops take their cue.
The earth spins in circles,
With laughter in every hue.

Flourish in a Floral Fantasy

Bees buzz like they're singing,
In their tiny, busy teams.
While the violets giggle,
Caught up in fragrant dreams.

A rose starts a conga line,
With all the blooms in tow.
As petals tiptoe lightly,
In a garden theater show.

Enchanted Garden Reverie

In the garden where gnomes giggle,
Flowers twirl with each little wiggle.
Bees wearing hats buzz in delight,
While daisies dance under moonlight.

A daffodil trips on a vine,
Spilling honey all over the line.
Tulips chuckle, their petals aglow,
As butterflies join in the show.

Worms wear spectacles, wise and grand,
Reading books in this funny land.
Each leaf whispers secrets, oh so bright,
In the garden of laughter and light.

With roots that tickle and stems that sway,
Every plant has a joke to say.
Sunlight giggles as shadows play,
In this garden where fun leads the way.

Flora's Graceful Mosaic

A peony pirouettes with flair,
Petals fluttering in the warm air.
Lilies leap over morning dew,
Sing a tune, bright and true.

Ferns in tutus twist and spin,
While thrifty tulips bet on a win.
Each bloom dons a smile so wide,
In this quirky flowery ride.

Dandelions giggle, seeds in flight,
Telling tales of sprightly delight.
With daisies drawing silly faces,
They brighten up all the right places.

And so in this garden of cheer,
Every bloom whispers, “Come here!”
Dancing petals, a jolly embrace,
Nature’s funny, floral grace.

Fleurs in Enchantment

In a realm where petals play,
Sunflowers make funny parades all day.
Violets wear shoes three sizes too small,
As garden beds echo their call.

Snapdragons snapping at flies,
Tickled pink, they can't disguise.
Roses tell jokes to make you laugh,
Offering joy on a flowery path.

Lush tulips turn their heads in jest,
Each bloom eager to impress.
The ivy winks, oh so sly,
While clovers dance and flutter by.

A whimsical breeze spreads delight,
As blooms bask in the soft moonlight.
Each petal a giggle, a story to weave,
In this enchanted garden, believe!

Swaying Stems and Starlit Skies

Beneath the stars, in a garden bright,
Daffodils dance with all their might.
Pansies prance, twirling with glee,
While fragrant herbs sip on sweet tea.

Cacti wear hats of glittering gold,
Sharing secrets that never get old.
With sprightly leaves that sway and shake,
Every petal gives a little quake.

Marigolds sing with a tone so clear,
While dainty ferns draw near to hear.
Fluffy clouds join the giggling spree,
Painting the night with wild jubilee.

In this realm where silliness swells,
Every flower spins its tales and dwells.
Under starlit skies, oh what a sight,
As the garden waves goodnight.

Petal Pirouettes in Twilight

In twilight's glow, petals play,
A dance of laughter, bright array.
With gentle sways, they lift and twirl,
Chasing shadows, a floral whirl.

A bumblebee joins the frolic scheme,
With buzzing notes that sweetly dream.
They tease the breeze with giggling flair,
As crickets tune their evening air.

With raindrops drumming on leaves so green,
The petals jump, a playful scene.
They tumble and spin, oh what a sight,
In this silly waltz of soft twilight.

The stars above begin to peek,
As flowers dance, all unique.
In moonlit mirth, what joy they sow,
Petal pirouettes steal the show.

Seasonal Sonata of the Blossoms

Spring brings giggles, blooms in a row,
Petals sway, putting on a show.
Summer's warmth, they bounce with glee,
A concert of colors, wild and free.

Autumn winks with a crispy beat,
Leaves join in with a rustling feat.
Winter chuckles as frost bites the ground,
Yet playful buds still twirl around.

Each season plays a different tune,
A melody sung beneath the moon.
From roses red to daisies white,
They dance with joy, a pure delight.

In every breeze, a laugh unfolds,
Every petal a story told.
Nature's choreography, sweet and spry,
A seasonal sonata, oh my, oh my!

The Tulip's Taunting Tango

In the garden, a tulip stands tall,
With a wink and a wiggle, it calls.
“Come join my dance, you roses so fine,
Let’s twirl and giggle, intertwine!”

The daisies chuckle, the violets tease,
As the tulip sways in the playful breeze.
“Who can outshine, who can outplay?
In this dance-off, come what may!”

With petals high and stems all bent,
They twirl and twirl with sweet content.
In a grand tango, the colors ignite,
A whimsical waltz in the soft twilight.

But oh, the wind loves a good laugh,
It sends them swirling, what a gaffe!
Yet in their giggles, they find their cheer,
The tulip’s tango, a dance sincere.

Symphony of Color in Motion

Start with a bud, a note so light,
Colors leap, what a dizzying sight.
Yellow, pink, and lavender hues,
A symphony dances, each petal anew.

They twirl in rhythm, a funny array,
With sunbeams as spotlights, they sway.
Each flower winks, a playful tease,
As butterflies glide with effortless ease.

The daisies sort themselves in a line,
“Come quick!” they shout, “It’s blooming time!”
In this concert, all take a chance,
With the breeze providing the lively dance.

And if you stand still, you may just hear,
The whispers of petals, so full of cheer.
A vibrant show, a visual treat,
In nature’s ballet, they can’t be beat!

Ballet in the Meadow's Embrace

In the meadow, bees do twirl,
With flowers dressed in a floral swirl.
A sunflower tries a pirouette,
While a daisy laughs, 'I’m not done yet!'

The lilies clap to a buzzing tune,
A rose flirts with the bright full moon.
Grasshoppers join with a leap and hop,
As petals shimmy, they just can't stop!

A breeze joins in with a joyful cheer,
Tickling petals, spreading the cheer.
The daisies giggle, swaying with glee,
In this meadow, oh what fun to see!

But watch your step, oh gentle friend,
A tulip might trip, it’s quite the trend.
As flowers dance in a riotous spree,
The meadow’s alive, and chaos is free!

Floral Duet Under Moonlight

A violet winks at a cheeky rose,
'You dance like you're wearing oversized clothes!'
While petals fluster, with laughter they shake,
Making sweet music beneath the lake.

The moon giggles at the budding affair,
As two blooms reach up to tangle their hair.
A dandy lion suggests a new step,
And whispers, 'Let’s dance, it's a grand prep!'

Stems twist and turn in the nighttime glow,
Ballet in blooms, a sight to bestow.
While crickets chirp out a rhythmic beat,
The flowers shuffle, oh what a treat!

But one clumsy petal falls to the floor,
And the rest tease, 'Just get up, let’s explore!'
Under the moon, what a sight to behold,
The floral friendship, fun and bold!

The Dance of Dew-kissed Blooms

With morning's light, the flowers wake,
Dew drops jiggle, what a fun quake!
Pansies prance in the early sun,
While tulips try to outrun the fun.

A dandelion leaps as a gust comes through,
'I bet you can't catch me, can you?' he cooed.
The lilacs laugh, swaying side to side,
'Let's whirl and twirl—come join the ride!'

With every petal twirling bright,
The garden bursts into pure delight.
Bees don their tiny, bug-eyed grins,
As petals pirouette in carefree spins!

But oh, look out! Be careful where you tread,
A sleepy bloom just fell out of bed.
They laugh and giggle, no need to mourn,
In this garden dance, a new day is born!

A Scented Waltz at Dawn

At dawn, the blooms are all aglow,
Joining in a waltz, oh what a show!
Roses glide, while violets prance,
With ladybugs giving a sideways glance.

Petunias chuckle as they tap their toes,
'Just keep your balance, or off it goes!'
A geranium shouts, 'Let's all do the twist!'
While cheerful daisies can't resist this mist!

Bees join in with a buzzing beat,
In this garden, it's really a treat.
Rainbow petals kick up some dust,
As laughter blooms, in petals we trust!

And if you step on a flower's shoe,
They'd say, 'Oh darling, dance with us too!'
As fragrances blend, in the soft light,
The blooms celebrate the fun of the night!

Elegance of the Tulip Twirl

In a garden, tulips sway,
A dance party on display.
Petals spinning, what a sight,
Even bees join in delight.

With a giggle and a fuss,
Watch them twirl without a fuss.
Each bloom dressed in fancy hue,
Shaking off the morning dew.

Dancing shoes, they've lost their way,
Tiptoe, tumble, come what may.
Ladybugs in fancy shoes,
Join the fun, they can't refuse.

Tulip twirl, what a delight,
Fluffy clouds in sunny light.
Nature laughs, and so should you,
As the flowers steal the view.

Fragrance of the Floral Waltz

In the air, a scent so sweet,
Petals join with twinkling feet.
Daisy leads, and they all follow,
With a wink, they lose their sorrow.

Roses blush, and violets giggle,
They dance around in a silly wiggle.
Sunlight shines, the shadows play,
A waltz begun, come what may.

Laughter rings through leafy halls,
As every flower bounces, sprawls.
Butterflies with tiny hats,
Swirl and spin with joyous chats.

“Step with me,” the pansy cries,
“Catch the beat beneath the skies!”
Nature’s laughter, pure and bright,
A floral show, what sheer delight!

The Rhapsody of Springtime

Springtime sings a funny tune,
With giggles bright as afternoon.
Frogs play drums, and birds will cheer,
A symphony of joy, oh dear!

Tulips bounce in joyful rows,
Joking round with pointed toes.
Windsurfing on a gentle breeze,
Each flower seeks a chance to tease.

Nature's jesters take the floor,
All the critters want to score.
With a hop, a skip, a bounce,
They twirl about, their joy announced.

Underneath the laughing trees,
Sunshine winks with perfect ease.
When the flowers join the prank,
Springtime laughs, oh, what a rank!

Choreographed by Nature's Hand

Nature whispers, “Let's have fun,”
Underneath the shining sun.
Dancing leaves and playful breeze,
Fill the air with joy and tease.

Wildflowers show their best moves,
Making paths and playful grooves.
Each with flair and style unique,
Turning Spring into a peak.

Pansies giggle with delight,
Swirling round, a joyful sight.
Dandelions spin and shout,
Show the world what fun’s about.

A bouncing bee does a jig,
With blooms swaying, feel the gig.
A dance so silly, never planned,
This ballet made by Nature's hand.

Tapestry of Leaves and Petals

In a garden where giggles reign,
Leaves twirl like dancers, a comical chain.
Petals wear hats that are far too grand,
Breezes tickle a whimsical band.

A tulip trips over a wayward vine,
Its stem gets tangled, oh how divine!
Sunflowers chuckle, a chorus of cheer,
Finding humor in blooms that veer.

Daffodils dance, their roots in a whirl,
As bumblebees buzz with a dizzying twirl.
Nature's own jesters, the colors collide,
In this tapestry where laughter won't hide.

So join in the fun, let your spirits take flight,
In this garden of giggles, everything's bright.
Each petal a punchline, each leaf a cheer,
In a world of soft chuckles, there's nothing to fear.

The Vibrance of the Fading Light

As daylight bows out for a curtain call,
The petals flicker, like stars after all.
Jack-in-the-box blooms pop out with a grin,
While shadows play tag, and the laughter begins.

A dandelion sneezes, its seeds take to air,
Making wishes and giggles float everywhere.
The fading light dances, a silly old sage,
Painting the petals with a comedian's page.

Butterflies blunder, their flight paths mislead,
Catching on edges, oh what a bead!
In the fading of light, there's joy in the sight,
A tapestry woven with chuckles of night.

So let's laugh through the dusk as the day comes to rest,
Finding humor in nature, oh, isn't it best?
Embrace every twinkle; let smiles take flight,
In the vibrance of twilight, we relish delight.

Graceful Leaps through Petalic Pathways

In a whimsical world of soft, spongy hues,
Flowers wear sneakers, ready to cruise.
They leap through the patches, skipping with glee,
Mimicking sprays from the nearby sea.

Iris tripped over her elegant trends,
And laughed with the daisies, such colorful friends.
Petals pirouette, while roots juggle around,
A ballet of blossoms, where joy knows no bound.

With each graceful hop, they scatter their scents,
Chuckling at grass that’s grown rather dense.
Their joyful ballet is a riotous sight,
Dancing through pathways, in day’s golden light.

So join their escapade, take a funny chance,
With flowers a-flutter, it's time for a dance.
In the merry midst of this enchanting spree,
Laughter and petals twine beautifully free.

Prance of the Peony Princess

In a crown of pinks, the princess does prance,
Waving at bees with a royal romance.
She twirls in soft petals, the air full of cheer,
While giggles erupt when they tickle her ear.

The daisies all whisper their well-practiced jokes,
But her poise keeps her rolling, a princess who croaks.
With pollen confetti, they celebrate right,
In the garden's grand ball, 'neath the moon's silver light.

Like a sassy red tulip, she teeters with flair,
But she stumbles and tumbles without any care.
With each little flop, the blooms burst with glee,
Creating a scene, joyous as can be.

Ah, prance little princess, adorned in delight,
Each flower a witness to your funny flight.
In this playful court, where silliness thrives,
The peony princess dances, and laughter survives.

Choreography of Blooming Dreams

In the garden, plants take flight,
Dancing leaves in morning light.
Sunflowers twist, they start to sway,
Bumblebees buzzing, hip-hip-hooray!

Tulips jump in a bright parade,
While daisies twirl, they're unafraid.
The petals laugh, a jig so spry,
As butterflies twirl and flutter by.

Caterpillars take their chance,
To join the fun and do a dance.
Nature's stage, a silly scene,
A waltz of colors, fresh and green.

Giggles float on the warm spring air,
As earth chuckles with a flair.
With every step, the plants conspire,
To put on shoes made of vibrant fire!

Springtime Serenade in Motion

A robin hops with rhythmic flair,
Singing tunes without a care.
While tulips tap their tiny toes,
The violets giggle, yes, they know!

Dandelions launch into a spin,
While clovers cheer from where they've been.
A breeze comes in, a playful friend,
It swirls around, the fun won’t end!

Picnics happen with cakes galore,
As ants arrive and start to score.
They dance on crumbs, a quick ballet,
Who knew a picnic could play?

As clouds burst forth with sunny laughs,
The whole meadow joins in gaffs.
Nature's rhythm keeps the beat,
Spring's delight is far from discrete!

Twirling Petals and Soft Breezes

A waltz of petals sways in line,
As blossoms giggle, feeling fine.
Every rose does a cheeky twist,
While pansies wink, they can't resist!

The breeze joins in with playful grace,
As flowers giggle, each in place.
Carnations shimmy, how they prance,
In this cozy, floral dance!

Grass blades clap with subtle cheer,
While ladybugs spin, drawing near.
Each flower knows their step so well,
In this garden, come and dwell!

Nature's orchestra plays around,
With laughter echoing from the ground.
Every bloom raises a laugh,
In a dance that makes each heart half!

The Dance of Colorful Awakening

Awakening blooms in a vibrant stir,
Start to joke, then giggle and purr.
Colors splash like silly paint,
A lily's prank, oh how quaint!

In the sunlight, petals twine,
Joking with bees, in line they shine.
Buds chuckle as they open wide,
Welcoming spring, what a joyful ride!

Squirrels leap with acrobatic flair,
Chasing shadows with utmost care.
While flowers yodel, bright and bold,
Claiming spring as their story told!

As every bloom starts to take flight,
The season dances, pure delight.
In laughter's rhythm, we can see,
Nature's humor, wild and free!

Tidal Waves of Color

Dancing petals in a hue,
Creating rainbows for the view.
Flowers twirl, a cheeky sight,
Painting gardens, sheer delight.

Bumblebees with tiny hats,
Tap-dance on the sunny mats.
Sunflowers wave their golden crowns,
While daisies turn and spin around.

Laughing leaves in breezy prance,
Scheduling a vibrant dance.
Silly stems begin to sway,
Cheering on this bright bouquet.

Colors bounce like balls in flight,
A riotous, blooming delight.
In this garden, joy unfurls,
With every laugh, a dance that twirls.

Dance of the Opened Blossoms

Giggles float on petals light,
Lively buds in morning's sight.
Rose and tulip, side by side,
Join the fun, they cannot hide.

Blooming friends with arms out wide,
Catch the breeze, oh what a ride!
With a chuckle, they arise,
Spinning under sunny skies.

Whimsical waltz, they sway and swing,
Nature's chorus starts to sing.
Each flower winks, then takes a bow,
Funny dancers, here and now.

With the pollen as their stage,
They perform with merry rage.
And as the garden giggles on,
Nature's dance will never be gone.

Soft Currents of Natural Elegance

The petals flutter, oh so light,
In gentle breezes, a pure sight.
Stems are swaying in sync with glee,
Nature’s way of saying, 'Look at me!'

Tulips tease with a playful bend,
Inviting laughter, a blooming friend.
Daffodils tumble, do the jig,
A garden party, warm and big.

Swaying softly, oh what fun,
Underneath the warming sun.
Each flower takes a little spin,
Chasing joy, they laugh and grin.

As petals pirouette in style,
The garden wears a cheeky smile.
Nature’s dance, so light and free,
Ensures that life’s a giggle spree.

A Symphony of Blooming Colors

In gardens bright, the hues collide,
As petals dance in purest pride.
Chirping birds join in the cheer,
Nature's band, come lend an ear.

With every note, the flowers shake,
As butterflies create a quake.
Cacti stand with prickly grace,
While daisies sport a giggling face.

As wind sweeps through, it starts to play,
Every blossom joins the fray.
With a wink, the violets sway,
In this floral cabaret!

Oh what joy, in colors loud,
The joyful bloom, a vibrant crowd.
In this garden, laughter reigns,
And happiness forever gains.

The Rose’s Regal Rumba

In the garden, they twirl with flair,
Petals spinning in the fragrant air.
Thorns gossip, oh what a sight,
As daisies roll in pure delight.

A bumblebee sporting a tiny crown,
Dances in circles, never a frown.
Tulips giggle, swaying with ease,
As the sun plays tag with a warm breeze.

The daisies chatter, their petals afloat,
While a crew of ants forms a funny boat.
A ladybug joins with polka-dot cheer,
As butterflies flutter, the show's premier!

In this ballroom of green, all join the fun,
With every last bloom soaking up sun.
A rose shimmies, oh what a tease,
In nature's dance, all move with ease.

Melodies of Spring's Embrace

Giggling flowers sing out loud,
Caressing winds, a playful crowd.
Silly daffodils sway to the beat,
While nature's rhythm shuffles their feet.

Breezy tunes tickle the air,
As squirrels join in with nibbles to spare.
A jolly robin hops and spins,
In this spring party, everyone wins!

With every bloom, a prank's in store,
While petals laugh, and the trees implore.
Caterpillars jig, flaunting their stripes,
In the spotlight of sun, nothing but gripes.

Nature giggles, her song so spry,
As buzzing bees harmonize with the sky.
Whispers of color in vibrant array,
In spring's embrace, come dance, they say!

Tidal Waves of Color

From the hilltops, colors wave,
As petals tumble in a floral rave.
A riot of laughter, the flowers collide,
Rolling downhill, let's take a ride!

Bright yellow suns and pinks conspire,
As wind carries giggles, lifting higher.
A clumsy bloom stumbles with flair,
Catching the laughs floating in air.

Dandelions puff, and seeds take flight,
Carried by whims, pure silly delight.
With each little pop, new laughs unite,
As colors leap, what a wondrous sight!

In this patchwork, joy reigns supreme,
Petal pranks are no longer a dream.
So gather your colors and jump in the fray,
In waves of giggles, let's all sway!

Harmony in Nature’s Dance

A field of green, a frolicsome stage,
As flower folk gather in playful rage.
Saplings sway, they swing low,
Chuckling softly, putting on a show.

Butterflies flutter, a swirl of delight,
Winking at bees in their bright-yellow flight.
Tulips twirl, their skirts in a whirl,
As petals prance, oh what a swirl!

A feathered cast hosts a lively affair,
With quips and cackles dancing through air.
The laughter of blooms, a musical spree,
With popcorn trees, oh what glee!

In nature's embrace, harmony sings,
As every last flower plays with springs.
With giggles and jigs, together we stand,
In our crazy dance, hand in hand.

Floral Dance Beneath the Stars

In the garden on a night so bright,
Tulips twirl in playful delight.
Daisies giggle, lost in the spin,
While moonlight laughs, inviting them in.

Bumblebees buzz with a little jig,
A rosebud trips on a stem so big.
With petals fluttering like a crazy hat,
They all take turns, what fun is that!

The willow shakes with a gentle sway,
While moonbeams join the floral play.
It’s a raucous scene of joy and cheer,
As flowers dance till the break of dawn, dear!

So grab a friend, join the fun,
And sway with flowers till the night is done.
In this merry garden full of cheer,
Dancing blooms create a world so dear.

Petals in Pirouette

At dawn, the petals stretch their legs,
And spin around like fancy stags.
They twirl and leap in the morning dew,
While giggling softly, 'Oh look, it’s you!'

Roses blush with a swirling twirl,
While violets giggle, 'Oh, give it a whirl!'
Every daffodil joins in the act,
As pollen drifts, not a single pact.

Tall sunflowers try to steal the show,
But daisies chuckle, 'Oh no, not so!'
With twists and bends, they laugh and shout,
In this rhythmic garden, there’s never a rout.

The lilacs wink as they take their turn,
Through pirouettes, they dance and learn.
In this flowery fight for floor space grand,
Every bloom spreads joy across the land.

Dance of the Flower Maidens

The flower maidens gather round,
Wearing crowns of green, so proud!
With giggles soft and feet so light,
They leap and twirl under the moonlight.

Carnations offer their fragrant flare,
While pansies promise to take great care.
In skirts of petals, they jump and sway,
Pulling daisies in for a frilly ballet.

In every step, they leave a trail,
Of laughter, love, and sweet-smelling gale.
With every spin, a rumor grows,
That they're the stars of this garden show!

For when the night brings twinkling sights,
These flower maidens dance in the lights.
With petals flying, the fun won't cease,
As they parade through the night in peace.

Whispers from the Garden Stage

From petals soft, a secret spreads,
A waltz of whispers circles their heads.
Each bloom has tales of laughter past,
They dance along, free at last!

Tulips tease with their daring flips,
While snapdragons take gentle sips.
With every twist, stories unwind,
In this floral show, joy's defined.

The daisies snicker as lilies sway,
'You call that a dance? Now, watch us play!'
With supple grace, they take their stance,
In a twirling chaos, there's no chance to glance.

So linger awhile in this vibrant glade,
Where petals gossip and fine moves are staged.
Let the humor of blooms fill you with glee,
As they pirouette, oh so merrily!

Petal Pas de Deux at Dawn

In the morning light they sway,
Two flowers waltz, come join their play.
With a giggle, one takes a leap,
While the other turns in a sleepy sweep.

The bees are buzzing, in a flurry,
Should they dance? Oh, don't you worry!
With every twirl, they chase a breeze,
Spinning petals, oh what a tease!

A squirrel laughs from a branch up high,
"Look at them, what a clumsy fly!"
The flowers blush, a bright bouquet,
As they keep dancing, come what may.

With each pirouette, pollen does fall,
A ballet that enthralls us all.
As dawn breaks wide and the sun peeks through,
They've budgeted time just for a few.

Spring's Captivating Crescendo

Up on the stage, the green leaves twirl,
While daisies giggle in a floral whirl.
The daffodils laugh, their heads held high,
In this spring frolic, they reach for the sky.

A ladybug hops, oh what a sight,
Dancing in circles, it feels so right!
With each little jig, she twinkles and glows,
Guess who's next? The snails in toe-to-toe!

The bunnies join in, with hops all around,
While the petals laugh, oh what a sound!
Each leaf does a twist, each root a glide,
In this garden gathering, there’s nothing to hide.

“Watch out!” cries the tulip, as birds take their flight,
“Don’t steal our spotlight, it’s our night!”
But chaos is charming, they all do agree,
Spring's grand overture, wild, wild and free!

Dance of the Golden Marigolds

Marigolds shimmer, like stars in the sun,
They sway in rhythm, oh what fun!
Each petal's a dancer, golden and bright,
With a crisscross of colors, a breathtaking sight.

The wind blows gently, a whimsical tune,
As the marigolds giggle, they'll dance till noon.
A cricket in audience, starts to tap,
With the quickness of feet, he joins in the clap.

And when the sun sets, they throw out a challenge,
"Can you keep up? Our moves are quite balanced!"
With spins and twirls, they wink and they flap,
Even the roses, start to fall in their trap.

As dusk settles in, they strike their pose,
The flowers all giggle, as moonlight glows.
Who knew flowers had moves so refined?
Marigolds of canvas, laughter intertwined!

The Enchanted Garden's Performance

In a realm where the daisies play pretend,
The garden hosts a show, a nature send!
Each bloom takes stage, with voices so sweet,
Competing for glory, a flower feat.

A tulip performs with a dramatic flair,
While a bold dandelion takes to the air.
The sunflowers cheer with faces so wide,
For every misstep, it's laughter, not pride.

The hedgehogs roll on, in the front row seats,
While ladybugs joyfully sound the beats.
With acorn hats, they clap and they cheer,
Through giggles and snorts, their joy's sincere.

And as the finale unfolds to the night,
A glowworm's dance shifts the stars to light.
The garden, a canvas, bursting with glee,
Nature's weird circus, forever free!

Sway of the Daffodil Dreamers

In yellow hats, they twirl around,
With giggles bursting from the ground.
Each petal's dance, a silly jig,
As bees join in, and start to dig.

The sunbeams tickle all their toes,
As butterflies perform their shows.
They flap and spin, what a delight,
With all the flowers, soft and bright.

Garden Serenade in Motion

A tulip sings in hues of red,
While daisies hum, and leap instead.
They tap their roots upon the soil,
In fits of laughter, dance and toil.

The marigolds wear hats so grand,
As violets flash their little band.
They prance along with joyous glee,
In this sweet spot of jubilee.

The Lilac's Lyrical Leap

Lilacs leap with rhythmic flair,
Swinging wildly through the air.
They don their sneakers, bright and bold,
And talk of legends yet untold.

A bit of breeze makes petals sway,
As bees do cheer, hip-hip-hooray!
With each sweet note, they catch the eye,
In whimsical leaps that touch the sky.

Rhythms of the Blooming Field

In fields of colors, all around,
A chorus of plants, a joyful sound.
They sway to music only they know,
In perfect sync, putting on a show.

The daisies wear their polka dots,
While sunflowers smile with funny thoughts.
A raucous festival they create,
As laughter blooms—it's never late!

Fluttering Petals of Grace

In a breezy dance, they twirl and sway,
Petals giggle in the sunshine ray.
Tiny dancers on a fragrant stage,
Nature's humor, quite the amusing page.

A butterfly trips, what a funny sight,
Stumbling over blooms, it takes flight.
With floral giggles and a playful breeze,
Waltzing petals bring joy with ease.

A Garden's Graceful Reverie

A sunflower grins, standing tall and bright,
While daisies gossip from morning to night.
The tulips wave, in silly formation,
As bees keep buzzing—their buzz is sensation!

A quirky gnome joins the flowery fun,
Juggling green beans under the sun.
They share laughs with shadows that flutter,
In this garden of glee, nothing's a shutout.

Choreography of the Sunlit Blooms

Dancing in circles, each flower pranced,
Determined blossoms, in mischief they danced.
The lilacs blew kisses, the violets clapped,
While petals formed shapes in the rhythmic flap.

A rogue wind giggles, causing a ruckus,
Spinning the blooms, oh, what a circus!
They tiptoe on stem, then leap to the sky,
With laughter erupting, as they leap high.

The Ballet of Vibrant Petals

Beneath a bright canopy, colors collide,
Each flower a dancer, with humor and pride.
The roses whispered secrets, so sly and sweet,
While peonies pirouetted with dainty feet.

A clown-faced bumblebee buzzed in the air,
Twirling and swirling, without a care.
In this comical scene, nature's delight,
Petals wiggled and giggled through day and night.

Nature’s Dance of Renewal

In gardens wide, where critters prance,
The flowers wiggle, join the dance.
Bees in top hats, buzzing cheer,
They tango through the petals near.

With butterflies on tiny toes,
They twirl and spin where sunlight glows.
A squirrel jives, not missing a beat,
While worms are shuffling under feet.

The trees all sway, a leafy cheer,
They laugh and rustle, 'Spring is here!'
While clouds above throw confetti down,
Nature's party wears a crown.

So join the fun, don’t be a bore,
Let’s picnic where the wild things soar.
A dance of joy, so light, so free,
In this merry garden jubilee.

Harmonies of Growth and Grace

With every bud, a giggle springs,
As flowers hum delightful things.
A daffodil dons shades of bright,
While tulips strike a pose, what a sight!

The sun winks down with golden rays,
While daisies show off in silly ways.
A robin chirps a goofy tune,
As bees respond, 'We're here till noon!'

Each sprout and leaf in wild parade,
They stomp and sway, a floral charade.
With Nature's hands, they spin and sway,
Creating art through dirt and play.

So take a step, and join their shove,
Make merry sounds, give them a shove!
In every tumbler, laugh and twirl,
Nature's concert starts to unfurl.

Ballet of Dew-Kissed Mornings

Awake with giggles, dew on grass,
The morning light brings blooms en masse.
A lily leaps with all its might,
While daisies chuckle in delight.

With shoes of mist, they glide along,
The croaky frogs join in with song.
A butterfly bows, then takes a spin,
While all the flowers cheer, 'Let’s begin!'

The sun peeks out, a spotlight bright,
While shadows dance and take to flight.
Squirrels take a twirl, they bounce and leap,
While sleepy bugs still try to sleep.

So let’s embrace this morning grace,
With giggling life all in one place.
In dewy gardens, laughter blooms,
As nature waltzes, cheerfully zooms.

Swirls of Fragrance and Light

In fragrant circles, scents collide,
The petals whirl, a merry ride.
A cherry pie of colors bright,
As scents of mint and thyme take flight.

The roses wink, they throw a prank,
Whispering secrets, giggles rank.
While bees take part in buzzing games,
The marigolds call out their names.

With every twist, the air grows thick,
A mustard yellow, a lavender slick.
Nature's circus, a whimsical sight,
As petals waltz, oh what a delight!

So breathe in deep, enjoy the fun,
Each fragrant moment, a glorious run.
In gardens grand, where laughter ignites,
The world's a stage of colors and lights.

Starlight Soirée among the Blooms

In the garden dance, flowers prance,
Petals swirling in a breezy trance.
Bees in tuxedos, buzzing with glee,
Throwing a ball, just wait and see!

Daisies giggle, tulips twirl,
Rose petals spin in a fragrant whirl.
Frogs in hats croak a comedic tune,
While the stars wink, under the moon.

Ladybugs juggle with such fine flair,
In this blooming bash, there's fun to spare!
Each stem stands tall, the daisies cheer,
As laughter echoes out, far and near.

So join the fête, let spirits soar,
In a vibrant dance, we'll adore!
With nature's rhythm, let's celebrate,
A starlit soirée that's truly great!

The Orchid's Opulent Overture

Orchids in velvet, oh so grand,
Strut their stuff, take a stand.
In this floral frolic, they flaunt their dress,
With winks and giggles, they pass the test.

Petunias pose like diva queens,
Flexing petals, it's true the scene.
A dapper snail slides in with flair,
With spectacles perched and slicked-back hair.

Bees now bob like they're on parade,
While ferns sway, a ballroom charade.
With glances shared and pollen tossed,
In this opulent overture, never lost.

A chorus of blooms, in harmony sing,
Spreading laughter, what joy they bring!
All together now, in this garden free,
Each petal a giggle, you must agree.

Chasing Shadows in Full Bloom

Under sunbeams, shadows creep,
In the meadow where silliness leaps.
Sunflowers grin as they sway around,
While playful squirrels leap from the ground.

A daffodil dodges, quick on its toes,
Playing tag with a breeze, as everyone knows.
Jack-in-the-pulpits burst out with laughter,
Winking at daisies, oh what a disaster!

Frolicking petals, all in a fright,
When shadows chase them, oh what a sight!
Laughing lemons, with zest they prance,
With silly shuffles, they join the dance.

Chasing shadows in perfumes sweet,
In this floral tale, joy's a treat!
Each giggle ripples, as daylight glows,
In a merry romp, where humor flows.

Midsummer's Serenade

Midsummer's giggle, where grasses sway,
Flowers hum tunes in their own playful way.
Willows whisper secrets to the bees,
As butterflies flutter, dancing with ease.

Pansies chuckle at the roses' plight,
When their thorns poke, oh what a fright!
Laughter erupts, across the green land,
While ladybugs join in, a jubilant band.

Garden gnomes tap their tiny toes,
To the rhythm of petals that tickle their nose.
Each bloom is a laugh, a giggle divine,
In this midsummer's show, everything's fine!

So come take a stroll, let joy lead the way,
In a meringue of fun, we'll twirl and sway.
With nature's gladness in every guest's heart,
A serenade of smiles, they'll never part!

www.ingramcontent.com/pod-product-compliance
Lightning Source LLC
Chambersburg PA
CBHW071839160426
43209CB00003B/356
9781805666479